MW00790352

THE PERPET
INCOME MACHINE

THE PERPETUAL PASSIVE INCOME MACHINE

A Proven 4-Step Process For Putting An Extra Paycheck In Your Pocket Every 30 Days

Jim Small Ray Brehm

CONTENTS

DEDICATION

This book is dedicated to all of the

brave children battling Rett Syndrome.

Please help them.

www.SecondChanceForSophia.org

DISCLAIMER

This publication is designed to provide competent and reliable information regarding the subject matter covered. However, it is sold with the understanding that the authors and publisher are not engaged in rendering legal, financial or any other professional advice. Laws and practices often vary from state to state and country to country and if legal or other expert assistance is required, the services of a professional should be sought. The authors and publisher specifically disclaim any liability that is incurred from the use or application of the contents of this book.

ACCREDITED INVESTOR NOTICE

This book describes an investing program that is available to Accredited Investors.

FOREWORD

KEN MCELROY

I have made it my mission in life to elevate the financial well-being of humanity. I do this through mentoring, speaking at seminars and authoring books. I also achieve my mission by connecting and building relationships with other entrepreneurs. Those relationships help everyone involved become more financially educated and successful in all of their endeavors. For me, those relationships include people like Robert Kiyosaki and Jim Small.

I've known Jim Small for close to a decade. We regularly spend time together discussing entrepreneurialism, real estate, and helping others. We both love the idea of helping others become financially intelligent and financially free. What Jim has created with SANTÉ Realty Investments is a company that teaches investors sophisticated investing and then does it for them.

One the concepts I am most passionate about, is the idea of investing for infinite returns. I regularly discuss it in my books or seminars. The opportunity in this book is exactly what I am talking about. "The Perpetual Passive Income Machine" makes such a great description. If all goes well, you will end up getting infinite returns and that is what every investor should be striving towards.

One of the things I appreciate most about Jim is his passion for life and giving back to others. He is very involved in his charity Second Chance for Sophia & Friends, as well as his educational seminars. He also shared his knowledge with the world in my book The Sleeping Giant, where he described a Higher Purpose, family and how building a great business is the best way to care for them.

My primary mission of teaching entrepreneurship is to give back to others. Jim does this by enabling other entrepreneurs and investors to leverage an existing system to strive for infinite returns.

What Jim has done with his SANTÉ Realty Investments 10-30 Plan™ as explained in this book is amazing. He has brought his years of expertise and connections, and made them available to everyone with a fantastic return.

If you're looking for a better way to invest, and in real estate in particular, this book will open your eyes to the importance of entrepreneurship, having professionals do your due diligence, and educating yourself with regard to the difference between return and yield. Don't just read this book once. Read it multiple times, until you have that "Aha" moment about this concept. Then go listen to Jim speak and explain it in detail.

And in the end, you have to take action. We need more sophisticated investors in the world. We need more successful entrepreneurs, especially those who are building streams of passive income. I love the idea of building "perpetual" passive income streams. So will you.

Ken McElroy

Ken is the author of the bestselling books *The ABC's of Real Estate Investing, The Advanced Guide to Real Estate Investing, The ABC's of Property Management,* and most recently his book on entrepreneurship:*The Sleeping Giant.*

INTRODUCTION

RAY BREHM

As an entrepreneur, real estate investor and relentless searcher for the best ways to produce passive income, I believe we all have two major challenges facing us. The first is: How do we build as many passive income streams as possible, and as quickly as possible? The second is: How do we avoid spending years or decades discovering the best sources of passive income?

Jim Small and I had lunch in early 2016. Ten minutes into that meal, we had exchanged notes and confirmed a simple formula for buying single-family homes. We had each come to the same conclusion on our own, over a period of many years and hard work. Knowing the content of just that ten-minute conversation can save anyone who is involved in single family home investing, tens of thousands of dollars in their real estate portfolio! The

1

information stored inside the heads of entrepreneurs and risk takers became my mission.

Another thing happened that day at lunch. We discussed Jim's SANTÉ Realty Investments 10-30 Plan™, which I had seen at his company's investor seminar, only a few months earlier. The more we talked about the Plan, the more I was convinced that I need to spread the message.

Jim and his company SANTÉ Realty Investments had already been using this investing method for years, but they were just starting to share it with new investors. It happened to be at the same moment in my life when I was making some massive changes and looking for secure, high-interest passive income. Previously, I had found that most "passive" income investments are not passive at all and often require all kinds of babysitting. However, for my plans, I needed an investment that was passive. My research has brought me many potentially passive income opportunities. These include single family residential rentals, business ownership, and hard money lending. I have also participated in more exotic things like REITs in Singapore and Hong Kong, buying digital assets (websites that produce cash flow), farmland in Chile, gold-backed lending in Singapore and wine cellar-backed lending in England. I was weighing all of these options for risk, return and how truly passive they were (I did not want to have to be involved in my future investments' operations at all!).

When Jim finished his SANTE Realty 10-30 Plan™ presentation, my mind was racing! We had been friends for a couple of years, but I never really knew how his investments were structured. I was excited!

I didn't sleep that night.

Here was an investment right under my nose that checked all the boxes for me. Jim had connections to the best possible properties in the country. The guaranteed income with his Plan crushed what I would guess 90% of real estate investors produce on their own (and with MUCH more work!). The investments entirely managed by SANTÉ Realty Investments, and therefore, truly passive income for investors like me.

In fact, if you look at what risky junk bonds are yielding (very low interest at the time of this writing), SANTE Realty's 10-30 Plan™ makes the stock market look like a joke compared to this type of real estate investing. On the risk side of SANTE Realty's 10-30 Plan™, the company takes on all the risk (borrowing the money) and the investor gets guaranteed "returns plus profits!" I knew that this structure was not something I could replicate on my own, even with my decades of real estate experience.

Towards the end of the presentation, Jim spilled a little golden nugget. I looked around the room, and since no one was jumping out of their seat with excitement other than me I was pretty sure I was the only one who caught on to it. This piece of information instantly became the focal point of the entire SANTÉ Realty Investments 10-30 Plan™. Many of the things that had been so impressive for me during the first 20 minutes of the presentation had suddenly moved to the back of my mind. But this one new concept was so compelling that I went to Jim afterward and told him he was under-emphasizing it.

Anyone who knows Jim knows he is very conservative in his claims. However, this was too big to understate. SANTÉ Realty Investments 10-30 Plan™ created a method whereby someone could conceivably invest once and end up with a growing list of assets producing passive income.

SANTÉ Realty had created a Perpetual Passive Income Machine!

Back at that lunch in early 2016, I convinced Jim to let me co-author a book with him about his plan. My audience is always seeking the best forms of passive income, and this was the best I had seen in all my years of searching. That is how this book was born.

The book itself gets right to the point, with no fluff. You will hear the plan explained in detail with Jim's expert guidance. The opportunity is for highly qualified investors only (i.e., Accredited Investors), but everyone must read this book. You may not be investing right away, but this book will teach you about passive income, real estate investing and even some incredible secrets Jim reveals about the stock market.

You will read valuable real estate investing advice. But mostly, the hour or so that you spend in this book will arm you with the knowledge that an investment like this even exists. That information alone will make you more informed than most investors.

If you are a business owner, and have been thinking about

building passive income streams on the side someday, you need to read this book . . . now! If you are a real estate investor, and are starting to realize the math doesn't add up for single family homes, which is precisely what happened to me, you need to read this book! If you have ever thought of investing in real estate, and don't know where to start, read this book first.

I believe this book is going to be a critical turning point in the lives of many who read it. Invest in yourself and read it now.

Success Always,

Ray Brehm

Co-author of the Bestseller: *The Soul of Success: Volume 2.* Ray's latest book is *Author Your Success.*

He is the Founder of **Dauntless Prose**, the publishing company that turns entrepreneurs into authors.

1

THE CONCEPT

This book is about real estate. It is about passive income. It is about education on one of the most important things that differentiate real estate (the way we invest at SANTÉ Realty Investments) and the way you might be investing incorrectly in the stock market without even knowing it. That difference is between "return" and "yield." The phrase, "What's your return?" manipulates us small stock investors. The establishment manipulates the use of the word "return" so that it looks good. However, somehow your accounts don't go up in value. Have you ever experienced that?

We're also going to talk about eliminating a bit of risk. Everyone always tells us in business, real estate and investing that there's risk. We are going to show you how we can minimize risk, and how you can rely on other

7

people to take a lot of that risk for you. Then we'll go through some ways to manage and leverage your retirement accounts, whether those are IRA's or 401K's. We'll give you some tips on how investing in real estate using those can be very beneficial. We'll talk a little bit about taxes. As boring as that may sound, it's critical because the difference between investing in a tax-efficient way and a non-tax efficient way can dramatically change how you live your life and how long you'll have funds in your retirement account.

We like to get right to the point, and this book is no exception.

We produce an average 10% annual return by investing in commercial real estate, and our investors get paid every 30 days.

That's what we do. It is a reliable, consistent income. It is yield and not return. That very important theme is evident throughout this book and in our entire operation.

A SIMPLE 4-STEP PROCESS

The idea behind the SANTÉ Realty Investments 10-30 Plan™ is based on keeping everything systematized and simple. The process has been broken down into four simple steps. As you will see, each phase has been well thought out and is led by experts in the field.

Step 1: SANTÉ Acquisition Advantage™

The process starts with the SANTÉ Acquisition Advantage™. Acquiring the right real estate is a numbers game. We analyze on average 100 properties for every one property we buy. That equates to us examining about four or five properties per day.

The first step in the process requires pouring through an

JIM SMALL RAY BREHM

extensive list of prospective properties. How do we find the prospects? We have a proprietary database of brokers all over the country that bring us deals on a regular basis. This database is something that took us years to build. It is not something that is available on the open market. We don't just google "Commercial Real Estate for Sale."

Brokers are always bringing us deals and many times we are some of the first to see them. In fact, sometimes no one else knows about them at all. That gives us a distinct competitive advantage because we can get better prices and we can negotiate better terms. That position means our investors also get better terms and make more money.

The time spent developing that database and investing in those relationships takes hundreds of hours a year. What happens over time, when you have proven you are excellent at due diligence and can close deals that perform, brokers will bring great investment possibilities to you first. That is where we are now.

At the time of this book's production, there were approximately 231 brokers from all over the country in our exclusive network all looking for the best deals for us.

Once a property passes our first stage, we move on to the SANTÉ Due Diligence Discovery™.

Step 2: SANTÉ Due Diligence Discovery™

Due diligence is where we get "boots on the ground" to do an in-depth analysis on a particular property. All of our core team members jump on airplanes and are looking at the assets.

Since we look at 100 properties for every one we purchase, we must do a lot of data crunching. There are many variables we are interested in for each market when analyzing an investment property. Many investors only look at price comparisons, but that is just the beginning for us. SANTÉ buys properties all over the country, and, therefore, we spend a lot of time looking at what matters in each location. Market demographics can make or break you. So, we start asking lots of questions. How is the job market? Is it improving? Is retail growing in the market? Either way, what's going on and what is driving it? It is imperative to know what the economy is like in those particular markets. It is our priority to know everything we can about the asset and surrounding area well before we present it to our investors.

One of the other top factors we analyze up front is risk mitigation. Many investors skip this part, or just do the bare minimum. We do a meaningful analysis here. The property has to be insured, of course. The property requires coverage for fire, flood, hail or wind damage insurance. But the mortgage structure is also critical. Exposure to any additional liability is not an option. Sure we want to make it, so our investors get the cash flow and the other benefits of the investment, but we hate surprises, so we take decisive steps to eliminate as many risk factors as possible. We don't want to take on any extra risk, so we structure and negotiate to minimize danger in all areas of the investment for our investors. That is a principal part of our methodology.

Step 3: SANTÉ Asset Management Method™

Post acquisition, we hand it over to our seasoned operations team. The SANTÉ Asset Management Method™ includes a comprehensive process for onboarding and managing a property. We maximize positive cash flow through the implementation of the unique methods that we have developed for managing assets.

Asset Management is the point in the process where we answer some crucial ongoing questions. Who will be used to manage the local property managers? When will we invest in new air conditioners? When do we plan to repave the property's parking lots? How often are we going to replace doors, fixtures, and faucets? How much should we set aside from cash flow each year for other capital investments?

We build a plan so that we know what we're going to spend every year on the property, down to the penny. Then, we are confident the asset will be in good shape 10 to 20 years out. That predictability reduces risk in the investment too. If you have ever invested in something, only to have someone call you and ask you to put more money in, then you know why we do all this analysis and planning up front. We don't like those kinds of investments, and we assume you probably don't either. That is really why the SANTÉ Asset Management Method™ exists, to mitigate risk in the investment.

Step 4: SANTÉ Investor Cash Flow Maximizer™

The last step in our simple 4-Step Process is the SANTÉ Investor Cash Flow Maximizer™, the most important factor of this investment vehicle. Cash flow is what differentiates us from other investments. We deliver bank account deposits every month to our investors. When we buy properties, we are buying existing cash flows. That enables us to begin providing income to our investors nearly right away (typically 30-45 days) from the closing of the property. Our financial team sets up the system that ensures payments are made to investors every 30 days. Then we look at how we grow the profits over time with a plan to improve those monthly payouts to our investors.

Each month our investors get a direct deposit and a statement. We have dozens upon dozens of investors getting paid every month. We have assets all over the country. We go where the best deals are, but to our investors, that is all transparent. As an investor, you get a statement and a bank deposit, without having to travel like we do.

The simple 4-Step Process we have described in this chapter is the foundation of the SANTÉ Realty Investments 10-30 Plan™. The plan, however, is only as good as the yield on the investment. In the next chapter, we will talk about how we find it.

3

FINDING YIELD

One of our network of brokers around the country will alert us to an amazing deal somewhere. We perform a comprehensive analysis of the property, and if it still shows promise, we will fly to the location to further assess the potential investment. We look to markets that have the right demographics and produce the best yield for our investors. As a Phoenix-based company, we would love it if we could buy all of our properties in Phoenix, but the yields we require are not currently available for Phoenix assets (at least not as of the writing of this book).

We invest only in strong markets where we can guarantee a 10% average annual yield to our investors and have consistent enough cash flow to pay them every 30 days. We are not buying assets in Phoenix right now because they're overpriced. It's just too difficult to get them here and deliver what we promise. Therefore, we jump on a lot of planes and go where the yield is. Nobody ever said that the SANTÉ Realty 10-30 Plan™ was an easy way to invest in real estate. It's just easy to be a passive investor with the hard-working team at SANTÉ Realty Investments.

Of course, we do own assets in Phoenix. Most of them were purchased five or six years ago when we could get the yield we needed to make the investment. Those yields just don't exist today. When the market turns down someday, we'll probably buy more here, but our approach is to look for stable markets and stable communities across the country, and that's where we go.

By seeking out the best yield available for our investors, we can translate their investments into immediate cash flow. We don't want investors to have to wait to make money (or receive their direct deposit). If you compare our investment strategy with others, say developing a storage facility, or building apartments or a retail center, buying current yield has a significant advantage. If you invest in those other situations, you have to wait for one, two or three years before you start receiving consistent cash flow. We don't do that. When we buy, we start getting income immediately. You always have to take that into account when investing, when and how you going to start getting your money paid back.

Our goal for each asset purchase is simple: we buy assets with existing cash flow. That cash flow must have the potential to be increased over time.

4

YIELD VS. RETURN

We hate to be the bearers of bad news, but the financial system is rigged. We are not talking about "Flash Boys" or anything sophisticated like that. The liberal use of one word is the culprit, one financial term that you hear every day. It is the one term that most people put the most faith in when evaluating the performance of their investments. That term is the word "Return."

The sooner you are aware of it, the sooner you will understand how to read between the lines and become wealthier in the process. Nearly everyone that has viewed the information contained in this chapter in one of our seminars has confirmed they had been duped by the financial industry using this term.

Have you ever been told that the stock market on average

makes 8% to 10% average return? Despite this, that 10% return somehow never gets to your bank account. Whether it's your 401(k), IRA or child's 529 plan, the returns claimed never seem to make it to your bank account or even on your account statement.

How can this be? We will let you in on the little secret.

EXAMPLE #1 – POSITIVE YIELD

Year	% Return	$ Balance
0	0	$100,000
1	10%	$110,000
2	10%	$121,000
3	10%	$133,100
4	10%	**$146,410**

AVERAGE RETURN: +10%
YIELD: $46,410

In this example, you invest $100,000, with a first-year

return of 10% which yields a $10,000 profit. So your balance at the end of the year is $110,000. This makes complete sense. The second year, you're getting 10% on the balance of $110,000 (or $11,000 yield) leaving you with $121,000 at the end of the year. The third year, starting with $121,000 and increasing 10%, you would have $133,100 by the end of the year.

The key to the calculation is the starting point each year.

In year four, you're starting with $133,100 and it goes up 10%, so you get to $146,410 by the end of this year. That means your yield becomes $46,410 in those four years. That's a straightforward return on your investment because it consistently produces a 10% return on investment each year. You don't have volatility, which is the SANTÉ Realty Investments 10-30 Plan™ model. We're always paying a very consistent return. And you're getting the yield that you're expecting.

Now let's look at Example #2 of our sample stock market returns.

EXAMPLE #2 – ZERO YIELD

Year	% Return	$ Balance
0	0	$100,000
1	58%	$158,100
2	-37%	$100,000
3	54%	$153,505
4	-35%	**$100,000**

AVERAGE RETURN: +10%
YIELD: $0

The first year your $100,000 goes up 58%. You think you have the best stock broker on the planet. So your account balance starts the second year at $158,000, but guess what? The next year it drops 37%. However, it is a 37% drop from your new balance of $158,000. So, by the end of year two, your balance is back to where you started ($100,000).

The next year (year 3), the market does great again. You

are excited. It goes up 53%, and your balance is now a whopping $153,000 at the end of year three.

But the following year (year 4) the market goes down again by 35%. Now, without looking at the example, guess what you've made in four years?

Nothing. Not a single dollar.

Your stock brokerage account will indicate an "average return of 10%" over these four years because they're combining these four years (two positive return years and two negative return years). When averaged, it is mathematically a 10% average annual return. But you didn't make a dime! That is incredibly frustrating, and we see it ALL the time.

Our last example, on the next page, represents the worst case scenario, which sadly has happened to a lot of people. See what happens when you have negative real returns and yield.

EXAMPLE #3 – NEGATIVE YIELD

Year	% Return	$ Balance
0	0	100,000
1	150%	$250,000
2	-20%	$200,000
3	-25%	$150,000
4	-65%	$52,500

AVERAGE RETURN: +10%
YIELD: -$47,500

You make a $100,000 investment in the stock market, and the market goes crazy. It goes up 150%. It is very, very rare, but happens. The market goes up high, and now you think you're a genius investor. Your balance is now $250,000. This type of gain occurred during the dot-com market in the late 1990's.

In fact, this high 1-year return has happened a couple of

times. At that point, you probably were told "Don't sell. You've got all these great stocks. It's going to go through the roof. Technology is the way to go." We find it interesting how, up or down, stockbrokers will always tell you to "stay in the market."

Back to our example, the second year the market dropped 20% (new balance: $200,000). The following year it was down 25% (new balance: $150,000) and then it finally went down 65% (new balance: $52,500).

Yes, after four years, an $100,000 investment yielded NEGATIVE $47,500, but according to the financial industry, this investment had "an annual average return of 10%."

Incidentally, on a 50% loss in an investment one year, it takes a 100% gain to get your investment back to the starting point. If that happened in back to back years, your account balance would be the same as two years earlier. Financial institutions will then tell you that you had, "an annual average return of 25%."

The way investment bankers, stock brokers, or financial planners usually get paid by charging fees, commissions and money management fees on mutual funds. The fuzzy math we just discussed is what investment bankers used to tell us not to worry. They say over time your investment will all average out, just keep investing. You don't get any additional money, but that you had "positive average annual returns."

We think this investing is counterproductive, so we came up with the SANTÉ Realty Investments 10-30 Plan™ with consistent yield, as in Example #1. We give investors a consistent 10% average annual YIELD.

5

WHY VALUE ADD INVESTMENTS ARE BEST

Commercial real estate investing is not flashy, it's just consistent and predictable. How do we invest in it? We buy commercial properties that will be predictable, reliable and that offers additional value in the end due to efficient operation according to our business plan. It's called a "Value Add Investment."

Let's show you what we mean with one of our properties. We found a 96-unit apartment complex in South Carolina through one of the brokers in our proprietary network.

This real estate broker told us, "There's this property that has a lot of potential, but had poor asset management." So, we flew out there, and we found out we could add value by implementing some of the best practices on our list. These are things like: increase the rent on lease renewals and adding utility income. Some apartments have separate utility bills for each tenant, but at this complex, the landlord was paying the utilities for the entire complex.

Here is what happens with tenants who get free electricity and water. There is no cost to them, so they run the water for 20 minutes before taking a shower. They leave the air conditioner on with the windows open in the heat of summer. However, by just implementing a $20 a month utility charge, this type of behavior changes dramatically. Our experience shows that by adding a $20 a month charge, we'll see a $40 a month difference in behavior. That $40 translates to cash for our investors, so we can do little things like this to put a lot more money in the pockets of our investors.

There were also a lot of pets at this property. The tenant demographic was one where many people had small dogs. They ran around these big open yards where no one charged for the dogs. We implemented a fee of $25 a month for pet rent.

There were playgrounds on the property, but they were showing their age. There were a lot of young families there with young children. We could get some nice people living in our community if we upgraded the playground, so we did that. That enabled us to increase rents.

The property had some signage, but people still had trouble finding the property. It was 90% occupied, but they had no sign on the main road. Many local landlords don't have the experience our team has, because getting a sign out there would seem like a no-brainer.

We did some other things to add value. We added some lighting and cameras. If you have heard of engineered hardwood, it looks like hardwood floors, but it's inexpensive vinyl. Once you install that, you can increase rents as well.

How about we add some new fixtures and faucets? We know we can get a nine-dollar light that looks like a $40 light if we buy them right. These things all increase our capacity to raise the rents.

This property had a lot of elderly veterans nearby, so we put in some handicap access. We had also noticed that there were a few VA hospitals nearby, so we said, "This is great. These are great tenants for us. We want to accommodate them." By making these improvements, the financials on the property changed significantly.

We bought this property for $2.8 million. SANTÉ brought debt (Sponsor Debt). We signed on mortgages of $1.8 million, and we raised $1 million dollars from our investors. Take a look at the summary of the River Oak property.

Property Location: River Oak, South Carolina

Value Add Items:
• Renew Leases
• Utility Income
• Pet Rent
• Replace Playground
• Add Signage
• Increase Safety
• Renovate 22/96 units
• Add Handicap access

Funding:

- Property Value $2,800,000
- Sponsor Debt $1,800,000
- Investors' Funds $1,000,000

Capital Investor Terms:
- Invest 35% of total capital
- Receive 50% equity ownership participation
- Enjoy 7% Preferred Return, paid monthly
- No obligation to sign on any mortgage debt

We sent out an email to our internal investor database saying we had this investment opportunity, secured the investors and we were ready to close. In this particular deal, we raised the money in about a week. Now that's very fast for us. Normally it takes a couple of weeks to raise the money. In this case, our investors put in 35% of the total capital, that's 1 million dollars out of $2.8 million. For that, they received 50% ownership. SANTÉ kept 50% ownership for bringing the $1.8 million in debt.

We also gave the investors a minimum of 7% guaranteed yield each year. Therefore, right away, even before we started raising rents and implementing pet deposits and everything else, we start paying investors a 7% yield knowing we're going to get to that 10% average annual yield shortly.

EXAMPLE #4: RIVER OAK, SOUTH CAROLINA

	Year 1	Year 2	Year 3	Year 4
Property Value (Beginning of Year)	$2,800,000	$3,270,000	$3,520,000	$3,620,000
Sponsor Debt	$1,800,000	$1,800,000	$1,800,000	$2,800,000
Investors' Funds	$1,000,000	$1,000,000	$1,000,000	$0
Property Value (End of Year)	$2,800,000	$3,270,000	$3,520,000	$3,620,000
Cash to Investors	$ 90,150	$ 137,400	$ 138,300	$ 77,900
Cash Yield	9.0%	13.7%	15.0%	Infinite%
Total Cash +Appreciation	10.6%	35.7%	26.3%	Infinite%
Cash per $100K invested	$9,015	$13,740	$13,830	$7,790

We know the property can pay seven percent, so our

investors began getting cash flow immediately. We also set out to minimize the risk, so we make sure that none of our investors have to sign for any of that $1.8 million in debt (SANTÉ Realty's executives do that).

This asset ended up paying $90,150 in the first year to our investors, which is about a nine percent yield. The property appreciated a little bit as well which equated to a total of 10.6% yield the first year. That is our type of boring, but straightforward and consistent return. How did we do the second year? Well, we were able to increase the rents and add value. Our asset management team did a great job implementing our business plan. The value of the property went up because of its profitability. Our second-year yield was 13.7% as a result of high cash flow and the property appreciated.

The value went from $2.8 million to $3.2 million. The property value increased because we raised all the rents. We also managed all those expenses, like the utilities, so the value went up even more. Our investors made a 37% yield in year two. If we were going to sell that asset right then, it would have provided a 37% yield that year alone. That may sound great, but we don't like to sell assets. The third year, we take the value of the property up to $3.5 million by continuing to do what we do best.

For an investor that put in $100,000 at the beginning of this investment, in the first year, they realized $9,015 cash. The second year, $13,740 cash and the third year another $13,830 cash. That's in their account. Meanwhile, we still haven't sold the asset. That's just cash flow. Cash flow is paramount to us.

Now the business plan is based on the type of mortgage we obtained. We can go back to our original mortgage lender. We say, "Look, the value of the property has increased. We got a new appraisal. We would like to give our investors their million dollars back, so please increase our loan balance and send us the $1 million." So by the end of the third year, our investors get the one million dollars they invested all back. Now they have zero dollars in the deal, but the profits keep coming due to their equity ownership in the property.

In year four, our original investors have been cashed out, but they'll still get a total of $77,900 a year (or if you're originally a $100,000 investor, you're going to continue to get $7,790 every year going forward). In fact, it might be more as we raise rents even higher. The main point is that now you have every single dime of your money back and you've been getting this cash flow since you initially invested.

That's the way one should invest. That's the way we suggest our investors invest in all opportunities. You don't want your capital tied up forever. You want to make your money and get it back (but keep the asset if it's still throwing off cash flow!). However, let's look at a little different example.

Property Location: Wichita, Kansas

Value Add Items:
• Playground
• Laundry
• Stairway Paint
• Covered Parking
• Signage
• Management
• Marketing

- Tenant Screening
- Utility Income

Funding:
- Property Value $1,800,000
- Sponsor Debt $1,400,000
- Investors' Funds $400,000

Capital Investor Terms:
- Invest 35% of total capital
- Receive 50% equity ownership participation
- Enjoy Preferred Return, paid monthly
- No obligation to sign on any mortgage debt

We bought this apartment complex in Wichita, Kansas. It needed a playground, as there was an abundance of children in the community and nothing for them to do.

We decided that if we wanted to raise rents and get families in these two and three-bedroom units, we needed to install a little playground there. So we invested in a playground as well as painted stairwells. We planned for some simple other enhancements, like adding laundry facilities and adding covered parking and signage. There was also this glaring lack of marketing for the property.

So we needed to do some better marketing and tenant screening. The previous landlords weren't marketing anywhere. They were just taking whoever walked in off the streets.

EXAMPLE #5: WICHITA, KANSAS

	Year 1	Year 2	Year 3	Year 4
Property Value	$1,800,000	$2,100,000	$2,500,000	
Sponsor Debt	$1,400,000	$1,350,000	$0	
Investors' Funds	$400,000	$400,000	$0	
Cash to Investors	$ 39,400	$69,700	$350,000	
Cash Yield	9.8%	17.4%	87.5%	
Total Cash +Appreciation	47.3%	67.4%	87.5%	

Getting the right tenants is one of the most important things you can do to add value to property. It is one thing if the property is "okay" and cash flows, but the property could perform so much better if the tenants liked the people living near them. They tend to take care of the property and are more respectful of each other. We had to improve the screening process of residents. In this case as well, for the cash flow to improve, we established utility income.

In this case, we bought the asset for $1.8 million. SANTÉ Realty Investments brought $1.4 million of the financing to the deal in the form of debt, and our investors contributed $400,000. This particular deal was a little smaller than usual, which benefited the investors as they only added about 25% of the total capital, but they still kept 50% of the ownership. The investors got paid every 30 days and did not have to sign on any of that $1.4 million in debt.

We won't walk through every detail on this deal's financials. But what we want to show you is how commercial real estate is valued. When you do an appraisal of a residential property, you can look around and say, "What is the value of every other house in this neighborhood?" That is not how it works in commercial real estate. Commercial property is valued on Net Operating Income ("NOI"). The bigger it is, the more valuable the property.

Two similar apartment complexes, located next door to each other can appraise differently. Commercial appraisers look at each property's Net Operating Income. That's the profit, so that is why we work to try and drive it up. In the Wichita Property, let's take a look at some of the details we did not show in the table. We pay the first mortgage of $93,600. Also, we have a preferred investor's yield of $28,000, guaranteed. Finally, there are some partnership expenses for doing things like the tax returns, travel to the property, and to set up the legal entities.

In year one, we had net cash flow of $22,800. The investors earn half of that in addition to their preferred return. That equates to investor returns of $39,400 the first year. They initially put in $400,000, so it's almost a 10% yield. The second year we did even better. The revenue went up by $50,000 (mostly because we charged utility income and pet rent).

Between higher rents and lower expenses, total NOI went from $165,400 to $225,900. Now remember, this NOI number is what determines the value of a commercial property. We still have the same mortgage payment, preferred investor payments, and partnership expenses. However, now we have created a cash flow of $83,000 a year.

Our investors made almost $70,000 in the second year on a $400,000 investment. At this point, we were looking smart in the eyes of our investors. It was at this stage, we made a mistake, but learned a critical lesson.

We sold the property and made the investors an extra $350,000 in profit.

Selling seemed like an excellent idea as we received an offer on our new (much) higher Net Operating Income, and we accepted. But . . .

The Goose that Lays the Golden Egg

Our investors got their original $400,000 back. They also received the first two years of cash flow (collectively almost $110,000) and then another $350,000 profit from the sale. That sounds like a great investment, right?

The problem is, we just killed the goose that lays the golden egg. Had we recreated the South Carolina scenario, we would have refinanced the property, given the investors their original $400,000 back and kept making them $70,000 a year for the next 10 to 20 more years.

This slaying of the Golden Goose is one of the most important lessons we have learned. It's great to have that one-time return and profit, and the yield was tremendous on the sale. However, we have disposed of an asset. It will need to be replaced and improved. That is when our investing philosophy changed. We learned that it is in our best interest and in the interest of our investors to hold the asset, return the capital investment to the investors and continue to pay yield.

This philosophy differs from most other real estate investors. The practice of creating value and then selling is the most common form of profiting in real estate. However, the productive asset has been sold and must be replaced. Most likely, the replacement asset will require adding value to increase profits. Here is the question, if yield is $70,000 a year and you have made back your original investment, would you be happy? The answer is yes because monthly yield continues to accrue.

In today's climate, we have banking relationships. Banks provide loans that meet our requirements and understand our philosophy. They know that we will hold the asset long term and that our intent is to return the original capital back to investors within a few years.

In this example, investors made an average return of 87% per year. The "aha" moment came when they started asking, "Can you find me another investment to invest in because I can't get even 10 or 12% per year elsewhere? Please find another deal for us."

We love the apartments. We love that we can add value rather quickly. We no longer like to kill the goose that lays the golden eggs.

6

WHY TAXES REALLY MATTER

In our seminars, when we talk about taxes and why they matter so much, we like to play a little game. If someone gave you a penny and then doubled it each day after that for 30 days, how much would you make? Well, today you would receive one penny. Tomorrow you would receive two cents. The next day, you would receive four cents. If you did not get taxed along the way, and it kept compounding, how much would you have at the end of 30 days? You would end up with $5.3 million.

See the table on the next page for the details.

ONE PENNY, DOUBLED EVERY DAY FOR 30 DAYS

Day	Value	Day	Value	Day	Value
1	$0.01	11	$10.24	21	$10,485.76
2	$0.02	12	$20.48	22	$20,971.52
3	$0.04	13	$40.96	23	$41,943.04
4	$0.08	14	$81.92	24	$83,886.08
5	$0.16	15	$163.84	25	$167,772.16
6	$0.32	16	$327.68	26	$335,544.32
7	$0.64	17	$655.36	27	$671,088.64
8	$1.28	18	$1,310.72	28	$1,342,177.28
9	$2.56	19	$2,621.44	29	$2,684,354.56
10	$5.12	20	$5,242.88	30	$5,368,709.12

Now let's take the same scenario, but introduce taxes. You are going to receive a penny on day one, two on day two, four cents on day three, eight cents on day four, but we tax you at 30%. You are taxed this way when you lend hard money. You get the interest and then taxed on that interest.

TAXING THAT SAME PENNY AT 30%

Day	Value	Day	Value	Day	Value
1	$0.01	11	$2.02	21	$406.42
2	$0.02	12	$3.43	22	$690.92
3	$0.03	13	$5.83	23	$1,174.56
4	$0.05	14	$9.90	24	$1,996.76
5	$0.08	15	$16.84	25	$3,394.49
6	$0.14	16	$28.62	26	$5,770.63
7	$0.24	17	$48.66	27	$9,810.07
8	$0.41	18	$82.72	28	$16,677.11
9	$0.70	19	$140.63	29	$28,351.09
10	$1.19	20	$239.07	30	$48,196.86

In this example, the tax bracket is 30%. A high tax bracket is 39.6% plus your state tax, and a low tax bracket is about 20%. When we apply the 30% tax rate in this example, how much will remain after the 30 days are up?

Astoundingly, that number is now only $48,000.

Your tax-free $5.3 million compounded becomes $48,000 if taxed along the way. The Same compounding, same return, but the taxes matter.

Let's talk about how this applies to real estate. If you invest and receive the 10% return we have been talking about, how does a couple of seemingly similar investments compare? What happens when you perform a hard money loan at 10% interest, or you chose to invest in real estate with SANTÉ Realty Investments at a 10% return? In the hard money case you got taxed 30% along the way, and it comes out very similar to the data we just showed you with the pennies.

When investing in commercial real estate with SANTÉ Realty Investments you receive cash flow paid every 30 days and due to the nature of commercial real estate investing taxes are reduced if not eliminated due to depreciation and other tax sheltering methods employed by SANTÉ Realty Investments. Much of the time it is when we sell a property (if you're not investing through a self-directed IRA or 401 (k)) that you'll pay tax on the profits. Even in this case you're still realizing much more profit than from a 10% investment like hard money lending or bridge lending.

Taxes matter. When investors come to us and say "Hey, I found this way to invest. It offers a 10% return just like yours. I'm going to put half my money with you and half my money with them." We ask them to explain the tax implications because most of the time they are not aware of it, and their return is going to be dramatically different, and the yield will be worlds apart.

7

A PERPETUAL PASSIVE INCOME MACHINE

The definition of a perpetual motion machine is "a hypothetical machine that can do work indefinitely without an energy source." This kind of machine is impossible, as it would violate the first and second law of thermodynamics.

A "perpetual passive income machine," would be the cornucopia for all investors. However, when we think about an income machine or a perpetual passive income machine, we just automatically assume that what we mean is that we are reinvesting our passive income yields. But the beauty of the SANTÉ Realty Investments 10-30 Plan™

is that it actually could become a perpetual passive income machine for you.

Your original investment creates a passive income. In roughly three years your original investment is returned to you. However, the initial cash flow (and ownership) remains. Now your initial investment can be used to create an additional income stream. Creating that new revenue stream is what is most exciting. If you spend $100,000 and earn a 10% yield, it is a great investment. Typically when you sell an investment, as we mentioned earlier, you have to go and find another investment. That capital needs to produce income. If, however, SANTÉ Realty Investments returns your original investment in roughly three years, that money can continue to build another stream of passive income without any extra investment on your part. The key element is that the original money just keeps building passive income streams on its own.

So let's just walk through a purely hypothetical, but possible scenario. You invest in a property and earn a 10% yearly yield for three years which is made up of a 7% preferred return and the additional 3% from profit due to equity ownership. Due to an increase in NOI, we can increase the loan and return 100% of invested capital back to the investors. At this point, the 7% preferred return ceases and all investors receive only a pro rata share of profits based on equity ownership in the property. Although you lose the preferred interest, you are probably still receiving three to five percent return on your original investment. It is amazing.

Let's hypothetically say that the investment never appreciates larger than the purchase price and your investment was $100,000. After three years you will have earned $30,000 in cash flow and be returned your $100,000 investment. If the preferred interest goes away, and the cash flow doesn't get any higher, you continue to earn 3% or $3,000 per year on the investment in which you now have no skin in the game. Someone else is managing it and trying to make it more valuable, as well as looking for that next property so you can do it all over again. If all variables stayed the same, and you were able to do it five more times, in 15 years you would have a minimum $15,000 a year in passive income without any skin in the game and without investing any more than that initial $100,000 investment.

You are handed a check back for $100,000, and you're

ready to roll it over again. That is why we call it The Perpetual Passive Income Machine!

8

BECOME A VIP INVESTOR

What is the best way to invest with SANTÉ Realty Investments? Become a SANTÉ Realty Investments VIP Investor™. Our VIP investors access new investment opportunities before everyone else.

Contact us to become a VIP, and start:

• Earning an annual yield of 10% or more on your investment
• Get paid every 30 days
• Risk mitigation through our proprietary processes
• Extensive, efficient property management experience
• A secured and worry free investment

Become a Santé Realty Investments VIP Investor™!

Contact Santé Realty Investments

Investor Relations

+1 480.398.4954

www.SanteRealty.com

9

FAQS

We have found many people have similar questions about **SANTÉ Realty Investments** and the **SANTÉ Realty Investments** 10-30 **Plan™**, so we have included this information here.

The pages that follow will hopefully answer many of your questions. However, we encourage you to contact us and ask any question you may have. Sometimes it is much easier to talk to someone directly.

FAQS

Once you increase the loan on the property and pay back the investors their invested capital, do they continue to see cash flow?

The answer is yes! We return invested capital, but your percentage of equity ownership does not change. You will continue to see cash flow after we have returned your principal investment.

At what point do you decide to increase the loan on the property?

It's really when that Net Operating Income increases enough where we can refinance and get at least 70% to 80% of the investor's capital back. It's at that point that we look at it internally and say, "Okay, now's a good time to return investor capital." We may not get 100% back on every deal. Some we do, some we don't, but it's usually 70%+.

What is the typical timeframe to return investor capital?

Conservatively we state at the end of three years. We tell investors it's not like a stock where you can sell it today, as it is an illiquid investment, but you will have cash flow from the beginning.

What are the criteria for selling?

We maintain and manage the assets as if we were never to sell. Realistically what we foresee happening is that as we continue to invest in larger assets, we will divest the smaller properties to allow our investors to "upgrade" to larger, perhaps more valuable properties. When we operate our properties, we manage them efficiently as if we're going to hold them forever.

At times someone comes along and makes us what we feel is a stupidly high offer and we sell, but we don't maintain the properties as if we're just trying to sell and get out. We maintain as if we're going to hold it for 10 or 20 years as long as our investors get their capital back first.

When the real estate market goes up and down, as long as you have cash flow, do you continue to hold regardless of current market value?

That's one of the things that differentiates us. Actually, in a lot of investment companies, they'll say, "Invest with us in our fund. We're going to buy assets. We're going to hold them for five years and then we're going to sell them." The problem is, what if the market for real estate is down in the fifth year? Their fund says they have to sell the assets and you get hit because they have to sell at the bottom. We don't have any such requirements.

Our legal documents say we can hold the properties forever, so we're going to hold them until the market's up and get the right offer, and then we'll sell. We are under no pressure to sell. We have cash flow, not only from day one, but we continue to add value to the asset to ensure that the cash flow will go up over time. People ask, "Did you get hurt when the real estate market went down?" and we can respond, "No, we don't sell. We have no pressure to sell the asset. We kept getting cash flow."

If investors get 50% ownership and they're not obligated to the debt, how does that work and how are you secured?

We structure these as individual partnerships. Everything is a private security, so just like you would buy a stock, we have a document called a Private Place Memorandum. Like a prospectus, it describes the risk factors, the company structure, and operation. Our securities council prepares the Private Placement Memorandum for each partnership. It is for the benefit of our investors and lets you know what you're getting for that particular investment. In general, when we find an asset, we'll take on 5-10 investors that make up that 50% ownership. So one might have five percent ownership, and another might have 10% ownership. Together the investors own 50%. SANTÉ Realty Investments guarantees the mortgage.

We secure investors by their preferred membership in the partnership. They have a preferred position to SANTÉ Realty Investments.

Our investment is not like buying a house. Our investments are in a partnership or Limited Liability Company that owns the property, and you're a part of that company.

Do preferred members get paid first upon liquidation?

The mortgage is in the first position. Preferred members are in second, and SANTÉ Realty Investments is in the third position. That's the security we promise in each of our deals; you get paid first.

How do you guys forecast rents in these markets?

Through our SANTÉ Due Diligence Discovery™ we analyze many variables and market comparables of direct competitors to the property. We look at the socio-economic trends for the region to develop an in-depth analysis of every property in which we engage.

Are these properties insured?

As a part of our SANTÉ Due Diligence Discovery™ team members get to handle a lot of paperwork with insurance companies. We have very stringent requirements from our lenders because they are secure, and want to get paid first.

Often they insure properties for two to three times what we pay for it. We just bought two properties in Tennessee, for $4.9 million and the insurance policy covered them for $13.8 million. If a tornado wipes them out, we will get a check for $13.8 million on something we bought for $4.9 million.

There is an insurance cost included in those expenses. We insure for events such as fire, flood, wind, and hail. On some properties, we carry workers' compensation insurance if we employ maintenance personnel. Additionally, we always have an umbrella policy for each property's partnership.

If you get paid monthly, don't you have to pay taxes on that monthly payment?

You would need to check with your CPA. We purchase the asset, and we depreciate it. The depreciation passes to our investors. SANTÉ Realty Investments doesn't take the depreciation. The investors get 100% of the depreciation until their basis goes to zero, and then it allocates to the debt holders.

You can only depreciate an asset until your basis goes to zero. Investors can no longer use the depreciation, so the depreciation reallocates to SANTÉ Realty Investments. You get 100% but only until you're at zero.

How are you different from a REIT?

There are two types of REITs, publicly traded and non-traded.

You can buy them in your Schwab account or E*Trade and go in and out of them in minutes. That is not us. REITs are publicly traded liquid REITs. There's also non-traded REITs, so that means they're not an exchange, but they're very similar. Essentially we are very akin to a non-traded REIT. Each property has its partnership structure, with its operating agreements, with its perspectives.

Taxation is different in a REIT. When you're in a typical REIT, you're somewhere between 4% and 7% return. Our returns are sometimes huge, but we average 10% yield per year so in general, we've got a higher yield. A publicly traded REIT is more liquid, our investments are not.

How often do you buy properties, or is it just dependent on when properties come up?

You are always free to call us and ask, but as of the writing of this book, we're on track for about $40 million of property this year, so that's roughly about ten deals. An average time frame is about every six weeks.

What is the minimum investment?

Minimum investment in most of our deals can change, but the minimum investment is usually $100,000, and you have to be an accredited investor. An accredited investor is typically someone who makes over $200,000 a year of income or has a million dollars in net worth or more excluding their primary residence.

What is the longest it can take to return investor capital through an increase of a loan? What is the shortest amount of time?

The shortest time to return investor capital is 18 months with the mortgage product that we're using. The longest time it could take depends on how quickly we can increase the NOI of each property. We do believe that three years is conservative and thus quote three years for refinancing. We purchase properties that have the possibility to be refinanced in the next three years, but cannot totally guarantee that there won't be an issue that will prohibit us from refinancing.

You mentioned that you would consider providing investors with a 70-80% return. Does that mean that if an investor put in $100K and you returned investor capital that they may only receive $70 – 80K back?

Yes. If you put in $100k, you would receive $70 – 80k back. Your $20-30k remaining in the property will continue to earn you a preferred return of 7% though. In addition to your preferred return, you keep receiving your ownership share in the profits throughout the life of us owning the asset.

10

ABOUT SANTÉ REALTY INVESTMENTS

The SANTÉ Realty Investments Team

One of the most critical things you can do in your investing career is invest with people that have experience. You don't want people learning on your dime. Let's just introduce some of the key players on our team.

Jim Small had a property management business that managed 2.5 billion dollars of real estate. That company spanned four states and two countries. The company signed on a ten million dollar account where it managed money for other people. The company grew for about ten years and then was sold to start SANTÉ Realty

Investments. Before that, Jim worked in a corporate banking and consulting.

On the operations side, **Jeremy Guay** heads up the asset management team. He's handled and managed real estate first in Colorado then Arizona and now in multiple states for a long time, so Jeremy heads up our asset management team. He flies hundreds of thousands of miles in any given year. On his staff, we've got local property managers. He's got asset managers, and he's got a whole reporting structure to make sure that those assets we buy are performing as we had planned, so our investors get paid, so we've got an entire operation around him.

Nathan Skankey was an executive for a Fortune 500 company, overseeing marketing. He's also been involved in family offices and investing in real estate his whole life. He headed up Latin American marketing for a large conglomerate as well.

We have a great executive team, all with lots of supportive people underneath them but this is kind of who you are working with when you are a partner with SANTÉ Realty Investments.

Board of Advisors

We also rely on appointed advisors. **Kevin Hardin** is our legal advisor. He's worked a long time in mortgages and real estate fields for a very long time, and we're able to rely on him when we've got complicated legal questions.

Scott Morrison, our CPA, heads up an accounting firm. As a CPA, he has three or four hundred clients that are in construction, so he is very experienced how to handle real estate from the bottom up.

JP Dahdah manages our strategic alliance with Vantage IRA, so if any of you have 401 (k) s or IRAs and want to invest in real estate, we have that relationship with this company to assist you.

Sometimes you hear that you can't invest in real estate in your retirement account and that's just untrue. You can, and our investors do it every day. We work with groups like this to ensure our investors can use multiple strategies with SANTÉ Realty Investments.

Jim Small, Managing Director

Mr. Small is the founder of SANTÉ Realty Investments and is responsible for setting its mission, vision and strategy as an innovative real estate company. SANTÉ Realty Investments currently has multi-family holdings in Arizona, California, Colorado, Indiana, Kansas, Nevada, Ohio, Texas, and Washington.

Mr. Small's background includes executive management roles with various family-controlled businesses and operations. Before starting SANTÉ Realty Investments, he founded, ran and sold his property management company in the southwestern U.S. Mr. Small raised millions of dollars in growth capital, systematized the business, and sold it for a substantial profit three years later. During his tenure at this company, he oversaw the property management of a 10,000 residential unit portfolio valued at over $2.5 billion.

He has been investing in residential properties for many years and holds an active Arizona real estate Broker's license as well as being an Equity Marketing Specialist. He has successfully closed scores of investment real estate transactions. Mr. Small also has real estate designations from National Council of Exchangors and is an Associate Member of the Institute of Real Estate Management.

Mr. Small has also performed as an executive for the world's largest corporate consulting firm, Accenture, while living in the United States and Europe, and achieved performance rankings in the top 5%.

His educational background includes an MBA from Thunderbird International School of Management where he graduated with honors and a Bachelor's degree from Arizona State University. Mr. Small's professional accomplishments also include the "Top 35 Under 35" Arizona Republic Entrepreneurial Award and the "Top 40 Under 40" Phoenix Business Journal Leadership Award.

JEREMY GUAY, OPERATIONS DIRECTOR

Mr. Guay has significant experience both as an entrepreneur leading real estate, consulting, and service businesses as well as extensive systems implementation skills setting up multi-state operations. His ability to ensure that proper controls and procedures are put in place to monitor and grow company-wide performance have resulted in multiple successful ventures Mr. Guay comes from a family of entrepreneurs, several in real estate, and has a bachelor's degree from Arizona State University as well as an Arizona real estate license.

NATHAN SKANKEY, INVESTOR RELATIONS

Nathan Skankey acts as the liaison for all investors by facilitating the process of investing in commercial real estate through SANTÉ Realty Investments. He has a traditional marketing background working as a brand manager for a Fortune 500 company as well as entrepreneurial experiences starting an apparel technologies company out of undergrad. Nathan also acts as General Managing Partner in a family investment office managing over $65 million in assets.

Nathan has an MBA from the Thunderbird International School of Management where he specialized in International Marketing and a Bachelor's degree from California State University- Fullerton graduating in International Business with an emphasis in Latin America markets. Nathan speaks fluent Spanish and is an avid marathoner and triathlete.

Steven Epps, Development Manager

Mr. Epps has extensive experience in Real Estate Design and Construction implementing over $150 million in Capital Improvements. He is a charismatic individual who has the proven ability to excel through innovative means of problem solving and team collaboration to ensure maintenance of the scope, schedule, and budget for various projects being implemented simultaneously throughout the country. Mr. Epps has a passion for real estate and entrepreneurial endeavors.

His educational background includes a bachelor's degree in Mechanical Engineering and a Master of Business Administration both from Clemson University. Mr. Epps resides in Atlanta, GA with his wife Liz and dog Jake.

ALYCE CONTI, MANAGER OF ACQUISITIONS

Alyce Conti has over 26 years of acquisitions and development experience. In those 26 years, she has acquired, underwritten and developed over 300 projects totaling over $5 billion dollars in value, comprised of hotels, mixed-use, retail, office, multifamily, corporate housing, industrial, residential, senior housing, affordable housing and transit developments. Alyce was the top producer at multiple firms developing real estate nationwide. Alyce most recently held the title of Vice President of Acquisitions and Consulting at Eden Development where she sourced deals, established market studies, performed financial modeling and secured debt/equity financing.

Alyce received a bachelor's degree from ASU and had obtained a Washington State General Contractor's License. While in Washington, she served as the Finance Specialist and Board member of the City of Seattle, Landmark Preservation Board.

DEENA HARDIN, ADMINISTRATIVE DIVISION

As a consummate business professional and powered with more than 20 years of successful experience in project management, operations, legal affairs and human resources, Ms. Hardin's background defines unparalleled service in operational management. Deena is experienced in directing effective inter-departmental programs and increasing revenue throughout multiple profit centers and operational business objectives. Along with her experience in consulting family-controlled organizations, Ms. Hardin's strong account management, and business expertise, with the ability to prepare and deliver successful business processes, brings laser-focused organizational strength to the operations and administration division at SANTÉ Realty Investments.

SANDI BIRKY, ACCOUNTING

With her experience in accounting and administration, Mrs. Birky provides detailed reporting and record-keeping to support the administrative division at SANTÉ Realty Investments. She carries a practiced knowledge of business operations due to her history in managing her own company, as well as other positions she's held in backoffice bookkeeping and operations. With this experience, Sandi understands well the underlying details in recording. Sandi's strong sense of urgency, paired with organizational discipline and accuracy add a dynamic of strength to the SANTÉ Realty team. In her spare time, she is an accomplished pianist and very involved with her church and with her grandchildren.

11

ABOUT THE AUTHORS

Jim Small

Mr. Small is the founder of SANTÉ Realty Investments and is responsible for setting its mission, vision and strategy as an innovative real estate company. SANTÉ Realty Investments currently has multi-family holdings in Arizona, California, Colorado, Indiana, Kansas, Nevada, Ohio, Texas, and Washington.

Mr. Small's background includes executive management roles with various family-controlled businesses and operations. Before starting SANTÉ Realty Investments, he founded, ran and sold his property management company in the southwestern U.S. Mr. Small raised millions of dollars in growth capital, systematized the business, and sold it for a substantial profit three years later. During his tenure at this company, he oversaw the property management of a 10,000 residential unit portfolio valued at over $2.5 billion.

He has been investing in residential properties for many years and holds an active Arizona real estate Broker's license as well as being an Equity Marketing Specialist. He has successfully closed scores of investment real estate transactions. Mr. Small also has real estate designations from National Council of Exchangors and is an Associate Member of the Institute of Real Estate Management.

Mr. Small has also performed as an executive for the world's largest corporate consulting firm, Accenture, while living in the United States and Europe, and achieved performance rankings in the top 5%.

His educational background includes an MBA from Thunderbird International School of Management where he graduated with honors and a Bachelor's degree from Arizona State University. Mr. Small's professional accomplishments also include the "Top 35 Under 35"

Arizona Republic Entrepreneurial Award and the "Top 40 Under 40" Phoenix Business Journal Leadership Award.

RAY BREHM

Ray Brehm helps his clients manage passive income streams and grow their businesses. As a real estate investor for over 25 years, he found the quality of good property management companies truly lacking. In 2008, he co-founded a real estate property management company and quickly turned it into a multi-million dollar business. Ray is also a Certified Business Coach. When you put the two together, that is where it gets very interesting. Ray has a knack for applying principles of good business to real estate. He also has a passion for helping business owners quickly convert their businesses into passive income streams. Ray believes "Passive Income is the Ninth Wonder of the World."

Ray graduated with a Bachelor of Science in Mathematics from Baldwin Wallace College in Berea, Ohio (now Baldwin Wallace University), where he was also a two-sport letterman.

As a business owner, Ray began learning and documenting what he calls the Mental Muscles of Success. By working these muscles, he found himself trying things most people wouldn't. "I went from obscurity one day to presenting along side with Dolf De Roos to real estate investors. I was coached personally by the founder of one of the top business coaching firms in the country," he explains.

In 2015, Ray became a Best Selling Author and advocate for entrepreneurs who want to write books. Ray co-authored *The Soul of Success Volume 2,* with Chicken Soup For The Soul's Jack Canfield and *Author Your Success* in 2016.

Ray currently assists high profile entrepreneurs author books through his company Dauntless Prose.

RayBrehm.com

DauntlessProse.com

12

SANTÉ REALTY INVESTMENTS' PROJECTS

TRACK RECORD

Led by Managing Director, Jim Small, SANTÉ Realty Investments has been engaged as a principal in nearly fifty real estate transactions. This experience includes the acquisition of properties such as those represented in the following pages. The list of projects details the location, purchase date, purchase price, current value, and Annual Internal Rate of Return (IRR).

PROJECT LIST

Junction Plaza Retail Center

Location	Indiana
Purchase Date	July 2014
Purchase Price	$3,901,500
Current Value	$4,150,000
Annual Yield	**14.0%**

PROJECT LIST

Watson Park Apartments

Location	Kansas
Purchase Date	June 2013
Purchase Price	$1,900,000
Current Value	$2,600,000
Annual Yield	**19.0%**

PROJECT LIST

Wimbledon Retail Plaza

Location	Texas
Purchase Date	May 2013
Purchase Price	$1,800,000
Current Value	$2,300,000
Annual Yield	**14.0%**

Project List

Mountain View Apartments

Location	Colorado
Purchase Date	January 2013
Purchase Price	$1,260,000
Current Value	$1,525,000
Annual Yield	**SOLD – IRR 40.0%**

PROJECT LIST

Ashford Retail Center

Location	California
Purchase Date	October 2012
Purchase Price	$5,300,000
Current Value	$5,600,000
Annual Yield	**10.0%**

PROJECT LIST

Chism St Apartments

Location	Nevada
Purchase Date	February 2011
Purchase Price	$499,000
Current Value	$540,000
Annual Yield	**7.0%**

Project List

Victory Manor Apartments & Self Storage

Location	Washington
Purchase Date	April 2010
Purchase Price	$1,050,000
Current Value	$1,400,000
Annual Yield	**18.0%**

PROJECT LIST

Rite Aid

Location	Ohio
Purchase Date	April 2010
Purchase Price	$150,000
Current Value	$250,000
Annual Yield	**16.7%**

PROJECT LIST

Willcox Gardens

Location	Arizona
Purchase Date	July 2011
Purchase Price	$135,000
Current Value	$160,000
Annual Yield	**18.0%**

Project List

Garden Apartments

Location	Tennessee
Purchase Date	May 2016
Purchase Price	$2,100,000
Current Value	$2,100,000
Annual Yield	**12.0%**

Project List

Plaza Court Apartments	
Location	Missouri
Purchase Date	April 2016
Purchase Price	$1,650,000
Current Value	$1,650,000
Annual Yield	**10.0%**

PROJECT LIST

Belvidere Square Apartments	
Location	Missouri
Purchase Date	April 2016
Purchase Price	$1,680,000
Current Value	$1,680,000
Annual Yield	**9.0%**

PROJECT LIST

Kingsport Manor Apartments

Location	Tennessee
Purchase Date	January 2016
Purchase Price	$2,300,000
Current Value	$2,400,000
Annual Yield	**11.0%**

PROJECT LIST

Westridge Apartments

Location	Tennessee
Purchase Date	January 2016
Purchase Price	$2,600,000
Current Value	$2,700,000
Annual Yield	**11.0%**

PROJECT LIST

Glendale Office Tower	
Location	Indiana
Purchase Date	December 2015
Purchase Price	$3,200,000
Current Value	$3,500,000
Annual Yield	**10.0%**

Project List

River Oak Apartments

Location   South Carolina

Purchase Date   November 2015

Purchase Price $2,400,000

Current Value $2,500,000

Annual Yield   **10.0%**

PROJECT LIST

Public Square Redevelopment

Location	Indiana
Purchase Date	August 2015
Purchase Price	$800,000
Current Value	$900,000
Annual Yield	**8.5%**

PROJECT LIST

Northside Indy Medical Office

Location	Indiana
Purchase Date	March 2015
Purchase Price	$5,700,000
Current Value	$5,900,000
Annual Yield	**13.5%**

13

CONTACT US

Become a SANTÉ Realty Investments
VIP Investor™!

Contact SANTÉ Realty Investments

Investor Relations

+1 480.398.4954

www.SanteRealty.com

Made in the USA
Monee, IL
21 March 2022